UNIT
1
BOOK 2

SRA Open Court Reading

Back to School

Grade 1

McGraw Hill Education

Program Authors

Carl Bereiter, Ph.D.
Andrew Biemiller, Ph.D.
Joe Campione, Ph.D.
Doug Fuchs, Ph.D.
Lynn Fuchs, Ph.D.
Steve Graham, Ph.D.
Karen Harris, Ph.D.
Jan Hirshberg, Ed.D.
Anne McKeough, Ph.D.
Marsha Roit, Ed.D.
Marlene Scardamalia, Ph.D.
Marcy Stein, Ph.D.
Gerald H. Treadway Jr, Ph.D.

Photo Credits

46 Steve Debenport/Getty Images; **47** Purestock/SuperStock, Inti St Clair/Getty Images; **48** Dex Image/Alamy, Wavebreakmedia Ltd PH27L/Alamy; **49** Steven J. Kazlowski/Alamy, Jupiterimages/Getty Images; **50** fatihhoca/Getty Images, Fuse/Getty Images; **51** EdBockStock/Alamy, SW Productions/Brand X Pictures/Getty Images; **52** Caia Images/Glow Images, ©Patrick Byrd/mylife photos/Alamy; **53** AP Images/Eric Risberg, Hemera/age fotostock; **54** StockbrokerXtra/Glow Images, Kobyakov/Getty Images; **55** Photopat/Alamy, J and J Productions/Getty Images; **56** Janet Kimber/Getty Images, Patrick Byrd/mylife photos/Alamy Stock Photo; **57** Dex Image/Alamy, EdBockStock/Alamy, StockbrokerXtra/Glow Images; **60** ImageDJ/Alamy, Eclipse Studios/McGraw-Hill Education, Hero Images/Getty Images; **61** Ocean/Corbis. **Back Cover:** Ariel Skelley/Blend Images/Getty Images, Fancy/Alamy, antoniodiaz/Shutterstock.com.

Acknowledgment

Grateful acknowledgment is given to the following publishers and copyright owners for permissions granted to reprint selections from their publications. All possible care has been taken to trace ownership and secure permission for each selection included. In case of any errors or omissions, the Publisher will be pleased to make suitable acknowledgments in future editions.

The Little School Bus by Carol Roth. Text copyright ©2002 by Carol Roth. Illustrations copyright ©2002 by Pamela Paparone. All rights reserved. Used by permission from North-South Books Inc., New York.

MHEonline.com

Mc Graw Hill Education

Send all inquiries to:
McGraw-Hill Education
8787 Orion Place
Columbus, OH 43240

ISBN: 978-0-07-667077-2
MHID: 0-07-667077-5

Printed in the United States of America.

8 9 10 11 MER 26 25 24 23

UNIT 1

Back to School

Book 2

Table of Contents

Essential Questions What kinds of jobs do you do to help in your classroom? Why is helping in your classroom important?

The Plant Monitor

by Michele Boston
illustrated by Sue Cornelison

Chapter One
Madeline

Every week Mrs. Bignall picked the class monitors. She always picked them on Monday. All the children got a job to do. The jobs were important to keep the classroom running smoothly.

Carla really wanted to be the plant monitor. All she had to do was give the class plant, Madeline, a little water. It was an easy job. Carla knew she would be good at it.

"Stacey," said Mrs. Bignall, "you can be the library monitor this week." She put Stacey's name on the list.

"John, you can feed Freddy." Freddy was the class goldfish.

Carla sat up straight. Mrs. Bignall looked at her.

"Carla, you can take care of Madeline," she said. "Remember to give her a little water each day. Maidenhair ferns don't like to dry out."

Carla was pleased.

Chapter Two

Too Much to Do

After lunch, Mrs. Bignall gave everyone a new project. Students had to write a report about an animal. They had only one week to do the project.

"I'm going to write about sharks," John said.

"I'm going to write about horses," said Lola. "I love horses."

Carla wanted to write about rabbits. The next day she brought her big book of rabbits to school and showed everyone the pictures.

On Wednesday, Mrs. Bignall asked the class for their homework. Carla hadn't finished it. She had one more question to do. She knew she would be in trouble if she didn't hand it in.

Mrs. Bignall gave the children time to do their class duties and clean their desks. Carla decided to water Madeline later. She cleaned her desk and finished her homework.

Chapter Three

Show and Tell

On Friday, John talked about his cactus for Show and Tell. It was very tall and very spiky. "This cactus doesn't need much water," he said. "It comes from the desert."

"Your cactus is cool," said Joshua.

"But look at poor Madeline," said John.

"That plant needs some water," said Joshua. "The leaves are starting to turn brown. Who is the plant monitor this week?"

Carla jumped up from her seat. She could feel her cheeks turning red. She had forgotten Madeline. She had forgotten all week. And now Madeline looked dry. The leaves were turning brown.

Carla ran to her teacher. "Mrs. Bignall, I forgot! I forgot Madeline, and now the leaves are turning brown," she cried. "Is Madeline going to be okay? I'm very sorry, Mrs. Bignall."

Chapter Four
Saving Madeline

Mrs. Bignall smiled at Carla. "Don't worry," she said. "I'm sure we can save Madeline."

She helped Carla cut off the brown leaves. Then they took Madeline to a shady spot in the corner of the class. They put the pot in a bowl of water.

“This will help,” said Mrs. Bignall. “There will be new leaves soon.”

“I’m sorry, Mrs. Bignall. I shouldn’t have forgotten,” said Carla.

The next week Carla was library monitor. She was careful to leave enough time for her job in her busy day. The following week she was a group leader, and the week after that, she was art monitor.

Then it was her turn to be plant monitor again. She was a little bit nervous. But do you know what? Carla did a great job!

Essential Question Why is it important to use good listening skills at school?

Story Time

by Margaret Matthews
illustrated by Marilyn Janovitz

Keep your eyes watching
and you will see
I'm choosing a book to read—or three!

Keep your ears listening
and you will hear
the words of the story in your ear.

Keep your mouth closed,
keep your hands to yourself,
so we can all enjoy
another book from the shelf.

Essential Questions Have you ever ridden in a school bus? What did you like about it?

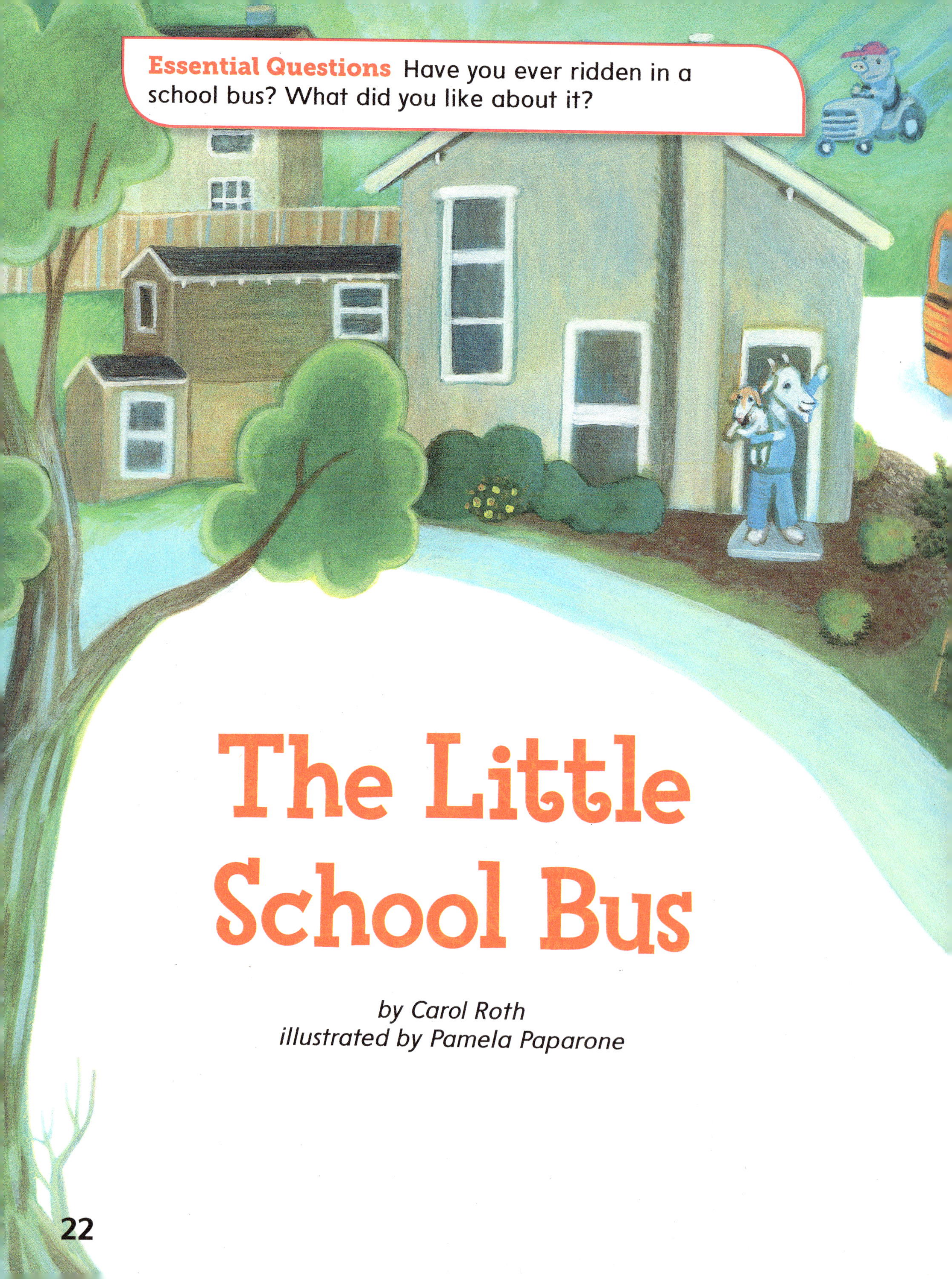

The Little School Bus

by Carol Roth
illustrated by Pamela Paparone

Here comes the school bus,
beep, beep, beep!
Step right up and take a seat,
and ride the bus to school,
to school,
and ride the bus to school.

The first one on is a little goat
wearing his new winter coat,
riding the bus to school, to school,
riding the bus to school.

The second one on is a pretty pig
and on her head is a curly wig.
A pig in a wig,
a goat in his coat,
riding the bus to school, to school,
riding the bus to school.

The third one on
is a sly, sly fox.
He has no shoes,
but he's wearing socks.
A fox with socks,
a pig in a wig,
a goat in his coat,
riding the bus to school, to school,
riding the bus to school.

The fourth one on
is a fuzzy chick.
She hops on the bus so
quick, quick, quick.
A quick, quick chick,
a fox with socks,
a pig in a wig,
a goat in his coat,
riding the bus to school, to school,
riding the bus to school.

The fifth one on is a hairy bear.
His messy hair is everywhere.
A hairy bear,

a quick, quick chick,
a fox with socks,
a pig in a wig,
a goat in his coat,

riding the bus to school, to school,

riding the bus to school.

The sixth one on
is a wiggly worm.
He can't sit still,
so he starts to squirm.

A squirmy worm,
a hairy bear,
a quick, quick chick,
a fox with socks,
a pig in a wig,
a goat in his coat,

riding the bus to school, to school,

riding the bus to school.

The last one on is a sleepy sheep.
She curls right up and falls asleep.
A sleepy sheep,
a squirmy worm,

a hairy bear,
a quick, quick chick,
a fox with socks,
a pig in a wig,
a goat in his coat,

riding the bus to school,
to school,
riding the bus to school.

During school
they learn and play,

while the little bus sits
and waits all day.

And when the school day finally ends,

the little bus starts right up again.

There goes the school bus,
beep, beep, beep!
Everybody's in their seat:
a sleepy sheep,
a squirmy worm,

a hairy bear,
a quick, quick chick,
a fox with socks,
a pig in a wig,
a goat in his coat,
riding home from school,
from school,
riding home from school.

Essential Question What type of job would you like to have someday?

What Will I Be?

by Jill Johnson

At school you explore many subjects. You learn about the world around you through science and math. You learn to share ideas through reading, writing, music, and art.

What do you like to learn about at school? Your favorite subject might be a clue to the job you will have one day!

Do you like to cook?

At school you learn about foods that are good for you. You might like to be a chef. They make food for restaurants and stores. You could use your knowledge about food to create healthy recipes.

Do you like animals?

At school you learn about different types of animals. You learn where they live and what they eat. You might like to work in a zoo. You could help take care of animals.

Do you like art?

At school you learn about colors and shapes. You draw and paint pictures. You might like to be an illustrator. This kind of artist makes pictures for books.

Do you like math?

At school you learn how to count and work with numbers. You add and subtract. You might like to work at a bank. You could help other people manage their money.

Do you like to write?

At school you learn how to write sentences. You use nouns, verbs, and other types of words. You might like to be an author. Authors write stories that teach and entertain readers.

Do you like nature?

At school you learn about trees and plants. You learn about rivers, oceans, and mountains. If you enjoy being outside, you might like to be a park ranger. You could help protect wildlife and where they live.

Do you like to make models?

At school you learn how to build with blocks. You fit puzzle pieces together. You might like to be an engineer. You can design buildings or machines.

Do you like to exercise?

At school you learn about being healthy. You stretch and use your muscles. You might like to be an athletic trainer or a physical therapist. These types of trainers help people move and stay active.

Do you like music?

At school you learn about sounds and rhythms. You sing songs and play instruments. You might want to be in a band or an orchestra.

When you grow up, you can do many of the things you enjoy doing at school. What job do you want to have in the future?

Essential Question What do you like to learn at school?

We Couldn't Wait

by Maggie Smith-Beehler
illustrated by Chris Lyles

We couldn't wait for school to start.
We couldn't wait to draw and write.
We knew that we would love to learn—
now here we are, and we were right!

We write *C* for cat and *D* for dog,
and show our teacher when we're done.
Each day we're glad for school to start.
We've learned that learning is great fun!

Glossary

A

active
able to move and have physical energy

C

careful
effort made to do something correctly, safely, or without causing damage

create
to make

D

during
at the time of something else

E

enough
the amount needed

explore
to look at something closely to learn more about it

K

knowledge
what you have learned

M

manage
to take care of and make decisions about

monitor
a person who helps teachers

P

pleased
happy or satisfied

S

squirm
to twist and wiggle in one spot

W

when
at what time